W9-DBU-081

Quarter-Peeled Oranges

Quarter-Peeled Oranges

poems by BRUCE GILLETT

illustrations by BILL NEEDS

Southern Lion Books   Madison, Georgia

20 June '14

To Rhonda,
all the best.

Bruce

First edition, second printing

Published by Southern Lion Books
1280 Westminster Way, Madison, Georgia 30650
southernlionbooks.com

Manufactured in the United States of America.
Design by Julie Allred, BW&A Books, Inc.

Library of Congress Control Number: 2011937584
ISBN: 978-1-935272-15-1

The paper in this book meets the guidelines for
permanence and durability of the Committee on
Production Guidelines for Book Longevity of the
Council on Library Resources.

"Poetry is an echo,

    asking a shadow to dance."

—Carl Sandburg

word-paintings of love

dedicated to

Dale

Contents

Acknowledgments

For our sons, Brent and Brian, who encouraged me to continue to write love poems dedicated to their mother, Dale.

For Bill Needs, whose heartfelt drawings expanded the imagery of the poems. Bill saw pictures hidden in words.

For JoAnn Dropp, my mentor, in whom I entrusted these poems for critical analysis. The mentoring sessions, that included push-pull when advice was offered about written intimate thoughts, will be remembered with gratitude.

For Marc Leftoff and Gallery Street, whose page and the giclee reproductions of art work brought the manuscript to life. Marc's late night hours were greatly appreciated.

For the artistic photography of Loren Haynes. Loren's photograph, "Passion," an anniversary card, set the tone for the poetry. And for Closerie Publishing, Inc. who produced the note card.

For Hank Segars and Southern Lion Books, Inc.; his constant guidance led the manuscript to publication.

For Julie Allred and BW&A Books, Inc.; her graphic design talent touched every part of the book, cover to cover; each page. Moreover, Julie's tender insight added much to Dale's story.

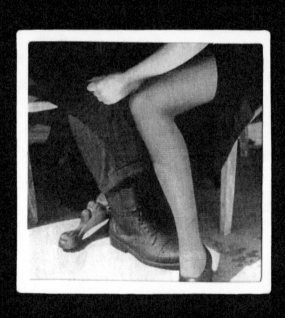

20 March '02

PASSION

Dearest Dale,

From the beginning at
the Sans Souci,
and forever,

I love you

B.

Introduction

Dale Pomerance Gillett, my sweetheart of forty-seven years, died of breast cancer last year, in our bed, in my arms. Forty-seven years, a flash. And afterwards one is left with soft clothing and heartache, and hard shoes and soft memories.

Love poems came into my brain mostly while in the shower. Five months passed, Dale's shampoo container at eye level, the shampoo with which I cleansed her hair as she craned her neck backwards; in June I started to write "Amaranth." It is odd that certain mementos of places and things and picnics and walks, stick in one's brain, when one truly wants to write of courage, kindness, profound kindness, beauty, grace, of loving and being loved. When one wants to tell that during Dale's seventeen year valiant battle against advanced breast cancer she was an inspiration to other women with breast cancer and helped them to become their own advocate; and to write that she was a collector, a resource of cutting-edge cancer data to share with others; and to recount Dale's spirit through the many years of chemotherapy when she said, "I may have metastatic cancer but I am ready to have fun," and off we went with a picc line dangling from her arm, extra Zofran, Heparin flushes, and other supplies—then the mind splits, the only image is that of our first meeting, Dale at seventeen wearing a powder blue dress, her hair chignon-style, blue eyes and that full smile, clear now as in the beginning—an easy to place be in these poems.

And so there are two worlds, one with remembrances clear or muddy, such as learning to make a French braid for a wig or learning the Vodder Method of Manual Lymph Drainage. A world in which the brain is scrambled, a disconnect between rational thought and emotion, yet these brain parts separated by centimeters conjure images and dreams. The other, is the here and now, of a heart cored out that can feel the hurt of others and embrace the joy of those who deeply love; the poems of love, loss and remembrance.

BRUCE GILLETT

I

Sans Souci Lounge (Romance)

You, my love, never ending vision
first as night glow outside the Sans Souci Lounge,
first kisses of full lingering honey—never enough,
blue water eyes glisten in the haze of lamplight;
now only the afterglow remains—never enough.

Young love at seventeen and forever
powder blue dress curving and clinging
embracing your warmth, your body; your hair chignon-style,
rhythms of love curving and clinging
and parking lot kisses—never enough.

We lie in a field of mountain grasses, feel the warm wind,
lightly touch the skin of each other.
We feel an electric tingle.
Is it felt on finger tips or skin?
My lips lightly brush your leonine brows
lips rest on your lids, brushing and touching—never enough.

Deepest love grows, a journey
of twisting rapid rivulets
that slows with time and trust,
waters merge, flow as
one water, deep, dark-blue; blessed—never enough.

Now my tears of remembrance are the only waters.
I long to care for you, to see you smile.
The promise of walking mountains in our eighties—a dream.
The joy of holding hands anywhere, everywhere, always attached—
    a memory.

Inscribed in your wedding band and forever etched in my mind
Ma Vie Mon Amour My Eternal Spring 3-20-1966

(28 June 2010)

Quarter-Peeled Oranges

Do you remember love and oranges, blood red fruit,
warm breezes above the Cornish coast of Spain, and below
lessons of love on the sun-seared sand, teacher of time?

We tasted their sweetness in the fragrant hills of Granada.
By the roadside you held an orange
and pierced the skin at the stem side,
your nails undressed each quarter carefully, tenderly.
My lips to your lips, orange scented.
My hands around your waist.

I remember love and oranges on the hospital balcony in Verona.
I gave you blood oranges to heal your paleness, while the
Sisters of Compassion cared for you, undressed your sheer satin,
and fervently dressed you in simple cloth.
You and sisters shared a knowing smile.
Warmth and sun, love and quarter-peeled oranges healed the shadows
     in your lungs.

Sleep my sweet, content is the water of Santa Margherita Ligure;
stars—souls of the night sky, are too distant to hear the street music,
too far to hear the bay water pulsate against fishing boats,
and too far to hear your shallow breathing—I am with you, I give you
     my breath.

My dreams were yours.
We awakened, we quarter-peeled oranges, and I kissed your breasts.

(11 July 2010)

Blue and White

On Poros, light heat rises softly and slowly in the morning
above our bodies and from the street below.
Breezes of salt sea air make gauze curtains dance
a white filmy ballet.

Afternoon white heat penetrates the blue framed open window
body to body, heart-heat sears within.
I taste the salt of love, droplets of love ... sweet.
While still, we see blue borders of white ceiling and window frame.

Sea air whispers songs, music from your heart;
we flow, undulate on wind-swept waves
blue seas rise and fall against
white stones and ancient broken marble columns.
Love and moon tides are constant and forever.

At Cape Sounion I call you Amphitrite dressed in blue,
your golden necklace glistens in sunset—*you are radiant.*
Your blue water eyes, deeper blue, always blue in my dreams
heaving waters below with sea mounds; seas of life, birth waters;
my love—*you are radiant.*

(25 July 2010)

II

Cancer

Tones of gray and sepia color the music of the cello
heard on barren rocks, faint sounds of sullen strings
turn your ear, you my sweet are sadly draped in black cloak,
I know your form through gray mist of song,
your silhouette and that within is beautiful and strong.

You do not turn from land so dour,
future uncertain, love's courage is strong,
you do not fear darkness of cello-made song,
or travelling gray paths to mystics and myrrh.

Tones of gray and sepia color the music of the cello
that sings to a breast and body diseased,
do not despair, you have my strength, you have my heart;
we'll travel gray paths for balsam and yew
hand in hand on this journey never apart.

Longest months of liquid poison drips, poisons the breast,
venom seeks your soul, toxic fluid seeps into the rest
of your body cloaked in darkness, eyes deeply set
sadly encased by a dark gray hue; eyes that do not weep,
I watch you breathe, I watch you sleep.

Tones of gray and sepia color the music of the cello
painful songs that furrow your brow in silence,
you do not speak of pain, or anger; you are frail,
please be well. I place my hand on your brow
I give you my breath, my soul.

Longest hours to slash the Peau d'Orange
and other sinews, in rooms bright white;
rooms light yellow where your lips smile, always
and sleep is quiet, you do not cry in the night.

Tones of gray and sepia color the music of the cello
sorrowful songs call from gray paths and
light green rooms and green-gray machines
that silently burn purple marked skin
and silently burn tissues deep within.

Tones of gray and sepia color the music of the cello
saddest of songs unheard by an innocent bride
dressed in Peau de Soie,
vows of joyous love forever.
Which memories to keep and which to hide?

(3 August 2010)

Saturday, 3:48 p.m.

I lost my lover. I am old and want no other.

I speak to you of joy when I see a young mother to be
then happiness when I see other lovers kiss;
it is for you that I smile when I see
an open hand that reaches for another, or
in symphony hall I see the couple seated next to me
holding hands.
You speak to me when I feel
the balance of love—caring and sharing.

I lost my lover. I am old and want no other.

You would have been sad to see a couple sit speechless,
stare blankly, joined only by the table in between
or when a vast chasm divided heart from heart
bridged only by Formica.

I lost my lover. I am old and want no other.

A thousand times a day I thought of you
during our love-life,
in my office or at the hospital;
I told some friends about the
momentary flashes of vision, or
an interlude hearing your voice;
they appeared bewildered.

On a Saturday at 3:48 p.m. I lost my lover
in our home, in our bed, in my arms. I lightly kissed
my lover's temple, that part where forehead met soft blonde hair,
and my lips felt her warm skin become cool.

You were as young then as when we first kissed.
You said, "Goodbye" the day before, and you smiled.

(13 October 2010)

Amaranth

I now use your Aveda Color Conserve shampoo,
in the beginning and through the end
the container half empty,
my heart filled with sadness;
empty.

I use your Aveda Color Conserve shampoo,
the container almost empty;
my love, are you amaranth?
You, my sweet, were the colors of my soul
purple, red, your heart and mine.

I used your Aveda Color Conserve shampoo,
container recycled, where?
My sweetheart—dead or amaranthine?
Everlasting fire burns in my heart,
bronze urn without a soul.

(16 June 2010)

Sweet Baby

Bitter orange, cinnamon, lavender, and lemon—
fragrant remembrances of you
linger on my skin
after my shower—
to keep you with me every day.
And I do keep you with me
as perfume of jasmine flowers and rose petals
that escape when I open the drawer
of hidden treasures.

I can almost feel the touch
of your fingers moving lightly on my palm
and feel those soft days and nights
when my fingers caressed your wrists.
If souls could touch, does touch remain
or go like wind blowing through grass?

Sweetheart, sweet baby,
it's so easy for my eyes to keep you
with or without music, they keep you;
and even without wallet-size photos
my eyes keep you;
and whether open or closed
my eyes see your breathtaking beauty.

(9 February 2011)

14

The Front Porch

Corner curves of cedar brace posts
that frame you in my mind
where we sat on rocking chairs I sit alone
and feel the empty time.

Red and white oaks whose leafy fingers sharp and round
join the sky and heaven above
my eyes picture yours
my life, my soul, my love.

Cedar posts set their roots on southern brick floor
strong masts firmly joined by handrails
form a sanctuary of beauty and peace
our blessed morning meeting place.

Oaks, *shumard* and *chinkapin*, surround our lives, our porch
never failing years of growth, their branches touch and
summer leaves brush each other;
your wedding band of entwined oak leaves
a band of trust—forever binds our hearts together.

Crisply colored autumn mornings, porch swings and rocking chairs
a new day, excitement, a new beginning with you
joyous mornings of fall warblers' song, music of our lives
memories of love still strong
roots deep firm and long.

Winter on the porch, bundled, hands warming hands
hot coffee-filled mornings, brown oak leaves still cling
to branches as undying love
hand to hand, ring to ring.

Your time of rebirth, scents of the spring
fragrances of sweet honeysuckle and daphne
of lemon and spice scented roses perfume the air
years of honey and bliss
each porch morning ending with a kiss.

(5 August 2010)

Clouds

Clouds (tethered to my heart)
above the Knowlton Meadow
(where I sit this morning yearning for you)
are gray textures of despair
that hardly move, anchored by longing.

Old magnolias edge the west side of the meadow
the east bordered by benches of remembrance
mooring love's memories.

A gray granite monolith
shares the meadow
with a loving sculptured sphere,
neither holds secrets
together they stay, day to night and night to day.

(15 October 2010)

Radiance

Drifting into another solitary year
atop Huckleberry Bald,
clouds, the mist of the Smokies,
were pierced by rising sunlight, painting
Turner-like brilliant nuclear flashes;
clouds and mist were fractured every moment
by the staccato of sunlit vibrant colors,
clouds disappeared, burned by rapturous light,
the whitest of white light soared heavenward.

(15 October 2010)

Claytonia Virginica

Come walk with me, my darling
on trails with hidden turns
on a bridge above the Greymont stream
by fiddle-heads of emerging ferns.
On a wooded slope toward Hooper Bald
I take you, March's Bride of Spring,
to find the carpet of Spring Beauty
and hear northbound warblers sing.
Come, my love, tightly grasp my hand,
to Haoe Overlook we'll climb
and rest amidst Crested Dwarf Iris,
the higher we go, we travel back in time.

Spring Beauty's pink striped petals give way
to seemingly random descent of leaves in fall,
yellow poplar spiraling down on a still day
is certainly not random at all;
or red maple that darts on a sudden wind
all follow paths to earthly destinies,
your favored burgundy dogwood leaves
cover footprints but do not cover memories
(Leaves feed the seeds of rebirth).

Journey with me, beautiful March Spring Bride
on high trails where trees rise to distant air
and worldly horizons vague.
Spring Beauty, stay close on solar winds where
(All is silent save for endless echoes of love).

(25 December 2010)

IV

I Danced With You

I danced with you, my love, tonight
on a Brazilian shore lit by candle light
and moonbeams.
Light danced on waters
to the ebb and flow of nature's music,
light of our love glistened, reflected in your eyes
soul-eyes streaming love-light;
your eye lids shadowed in purple, elliptical
and those lips, your lips, your smile that lit up my life
brightened countless rooms and the light of galaxies beyond;
your left hand graced my shoulder
my right—your waist
the warm air (part of our being) between us.
Your lime-green dress touched with purple ellipses
caressed your body, swaying
as we danced to Latin rhythms.
We danced, our bare feet scarcely an inch above sandy shore,
above water's edge and
glided above moonlit waters;
beauty, truth, ecstasy, paradise—never ending

I awakened
and formed your body with my hands
and caressed your lime-green and purple dress
and kissed your lips
and closed my eyes and danced again.

(19 October 2010)

Rainbow

Yesterday in The Temple a rainbow, white, ruby and sapphire
ascended the eastern wall as the afternoon sun wept.
Light of your soul, refracted through stained glass
entered the sanctuary, entered my heart-mind
and through a prism of chandelier above
you were there, the rainbow of your life, your love.

Your smile sparkled on the wall of life
sweet lips red as rubies, memories of sweet kisses
a glow of dazzling colors, you sparked joy
your eyes glistened as sapphires, soul searching
you found a place where heaven and earth touch
to know I loved and love you so very much.

Toward evening of peaceful blessed song
of quiet thought of present time
tears blend with the smile of smiles past,
the vision of your colors a luminous spirit.
As the sun sets to brighten hope in other space
your brilliance refracts upwards in elegant grace.

Yesterdays disappeared as the sun slept
the prism of your soul no longer illumined
after your colors faded into the sanctuary dome
your heart-light returned to your eternal home.

I breathe the air you breathed
I keep the light of your life in my heart
I keep your love … always have … always will

(19 September 2010)

North Star

Silence of darkness within the depth of space
where time moves ever slowly
and all memory erased;
is that the fate of all who lived,
dust designed for God or Godless place?

In the cold, cold distant space of time and before time,
time that was and time to be,
there are souls that linger and search, that hope to be lit by
stars of sadness that were and stars of sadness to be.

North star, fixed star, I see you clearly on cloudless nights
while others move about you, you are steadfast
during nights of despair and longing, loveless nights,
love no longer warm from candle lights.

From that universal beam, center of my being
and core of my heart, before and now,
a thought, a light, flows through pictures in my mind
to join my eternal love, I cross dimensions of dark time.

(28 July 2010)

V

Cyan And Teal

Warm copper curves, bend and yield
your warm body soft and smooth
(the curve of your back I loved to kiss)
bends against my body in the midst of our desire
in rented rooms at the Great Southern Hotel
where a light bulb dangled from ceiling cord
or in Pullman cars of the Southern Crescent,
sojourn: Slidell, Louisiana

Hues of fiery heated copper
glow and melt into amorphous forms
bodies flowing toward one another—inseparable

Aged copper garden arches frame our garden path
a canopy of weathered patina
years of love, of garden walks
under arbors dressed with 'Cornelia' musk roses
we planted and nurtured roses . . . each other

(*18 August 2010*)

The Fireplace

I lit a fire, the first this year
partly to warm friends
in part to rekindle memories
but mostly I made the fire for you.

Morning fires had meaning—
to light your smile, to warm your hands,
to comfort your robed body.
I split fallen oak, maple and hickory
to warm your heart—it was their purpose;
I was blessed to exist on this earth for you, too.

Evening fires were different, a luxury of sorts
for warmth was already ours;
an intermezzo between day and dreams.
Logs crackled, embers glowed and sparked a quiet joy,
an enchanting time to stroke your hair,
a time for lips to meet
for so beautiful you were;
to look deep into your eyes
content—complete.

(5 December 2010)

The Music Box

"Hi Sweetheart," the magic of your voice
sound of love I heard each day
on the telephone or at the open door
now quiet, whispers fading
into memory lost in time.

"Hi Honey," that same short song
of I love you
as it is inscribed on the glass music box

> *Today . . . Tomorrow . . . Forever*
> *I Love You*
> *Dale*

And sometimes I wind the stem and listen
to *Claire de Lune*
when I truly desire to rewind time
and hear music in my mind—
"Hi Sweetheart, Hi Honey."

(11 August 2010)

VI

Nana's Blanket

Most of the time the fuchsia colored blanket
that covers one-half of our bed
lays flat, quiet, perhaps asleep.
And before sleep, you smiled when you looked
through the bedroom windows a foot away
and saw the fuchsia blossoms.
You gathered scores of nearby camellia blossoms
to float in glass bowls for candle lit dining
and to celebrate love;
your touch of bright happiness.

You must know that your blanket awakens
when our granddaughters, Lucy and Rose visit;
they wrap and wrap their bodies tightly in your
fuchsia-warmth and soft fuchsia-love.

(29 December 2010)

Legacy

In the beginning
the heart opens suddenly
sudden as geological breaks
of youngest mountains
sharp, angular, restless lines
fractals, new beautiful designs
that worn by wind, water, time
become smooth, tranquil, fertile
a home where love breathes slowly
and air intoxicates and vines entwine
where vineyards bear the sweetest fruit,
a home where children sing with you
a wild child who can sing a song of love
a blue-eyed child whose gifts were notes
and the music is passed along
to children of children, some curly haired
a blending, almost perfect instruments
who sing verses with you—
and after the singing stops
the notes remain
the clearest of notes—imprinting
and so the music begins again
sung by children of children
songs for you and about you
songs of kindness, of courage, of love.
That which remains—echoes

(26 February 2011)

Still so beautiful after many years of chemotherapy, surgeries, and radiation